D1124507

Pebble®

Sphynx Cats

by Connie Colwell Miller

Consulting Editor: Gail Saunders-Smith, PhD

Consultant: Jennifer Zablotny, DVM
Member, American Veterinary Medical Association

Capstone
press®

Mankato, Minnesota

Pebble Books are published by Capstone Press,
151 Good Counsel Drive, P.O. Box 669, Mankato, Minnesota 56002.
www.capstonepress.com

1 2 3 4 5 6 13 12 11 10 09 08

Library of Congress Cataloging-in-Publication Data
Miller, Connie Colwell, 1976–
    Sphynx cats / by Connie Colwell Miller.
    p. cm. — (Pebble Books. Cats)
    Includes bibliographical references and index.
    Summary: "Simple text and photographs present an introduction to the
Sphynx breed, its growth from kitten to adult, and pet care information" — Provided
by publisher.
    ISBN-13: 978-1-4296-1717-8 (hardcover)
    ISBN-10: 1-4296-1717-9 (hardcover)
    1. Sphynx cat — Juvenile literature. I. Title. II. Series.
SF449.S68M55 2009
636.8 — dc22   2007051276

Note to Parents and Teachers

The Cats set supports national science standards related to life
science. This book describes and illustrates Sphynx cats. The images
support early readers in understanding the text. The repetition of
words and phrases helps early readers learn new words. This book
also introduces early readers to subject-specific vocabulary words,
which are defined in the Glossary section. Early readers may need
assistance to read some words and to use the Table of Contents,
Glossary, Read More, Internet Sites, and Index sections of the book.

Table of Contents

Hairless Cats

Sphynx cats look
like they have no hair.
They are called
hairless cats.

Say it like this:
Sphynx
(SFINGKS)

Some sphynx have
tiny hairs close to
their bodies.
Petting a Sphynx is like
touching a warm peach.

Sphynx may be
any color.
Their color shows
on their skin
instead of their fur.

From Kitten to Adult

Newborn Sphynx kittens have wrinkly skin. Their wrinkles smooth as they grow.

Young Sphynx are
playful and curious.
They have
a lot of energy.

Fully grown Sphynx
are medium-sized cats.
Their bodies are
thin and strong.

16

Caring for Sphynx

Sphynx' skin
gets greasy.
They need to be
cleaned every week.

Sphynx are indoor cats.
They do not have hair
to protect them.
They can get cold
or sunburned.

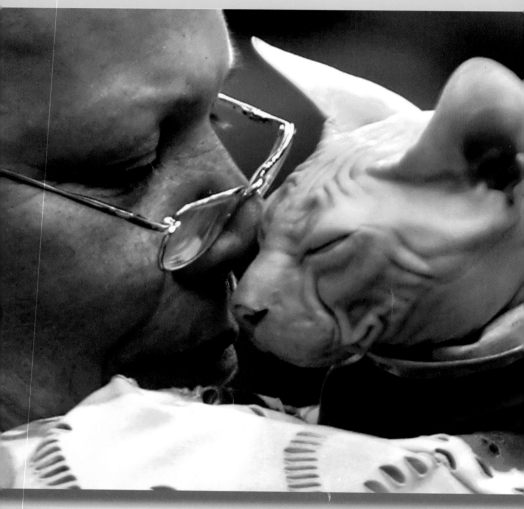

Sphynx make
fun, loving pets.
Their hairless look
makes them special.

Glossary

curious — eager to explore and learn about new things

energy — the strength to do active things without getting tired

greasy — shiny, wet, and oily

protect — to keep something safe

sunburned — having sore, red skin caused by staying in sunlight too long

wrinkly — covered with lines or folds

Read More

Barnes, Julia. *Pet Cats.* Pet Pals. Milwaukee: Gareth Stevens, 2007.

Shores, Erika L. *Caring for Your Cat.* Positively Pets. Mankato, Minn.: Capstone Press, 2007.

Internet Sites

FactHound offers a safe, fun way to find Internet sites related to this book. All of the sites on FactHound have been researched by our staff.

Here's how:

1. Visit *www.facthound.com*

2. Choose your grade level.

3. Type in this book ID **1429617179** for age-appropriate sites. You may also browse subjects by clicking on letters, or by clicking on pictures and words.

4. Click on the **Fetch It** button.

FactHound will fetch the best sites for you!

Index

Word Count: 122
Grade: 1
Early-Intervention Level: 12

Editorial Credits
Lori Shores, editor; Renée T. Doyle, set designer; Danielle Ceminsky, book designer;
    Wanda Winch, photo researcher

Photo Credits
AP Images/Dmitry Lovetsky, 20
Dreamstime/Richardpickup, 6
Getty Images Inc./Amana Images/Sante Milio, 8
Landov LLC/Reuters/Alexander Natruskin, 18
Nancy M. McCallum, 16
Photos.com, 14
Ron Kimball Stock/Ron Kimball, 4
Shutterstock/Anna Utekhina, cover, 1, 22; Mr. TopGear, 10, 12